THE INTENTIONAL DATING MANUAL

How to Date with Discernment, Boundaries, and Purpose

ECLESIA HOLMES

PUBLISHED IN 2026 BY PEN TO PURPOSE PUBLISHING, LLC

ECLESIA'S HOLMES
LINCOLN PARK, MI 48146

FOR PERMISSION REQUESTS, WRITE TO THE AUTHOR AT:
PENTOPURPOSEPUBLISHINGLLC@GMAIL.COM

ISBN: 979-8-9951413-1-0

COVER DESIGN BY CARAMEL XPRESSIONS
PRINTED IN U.S.A

Table of Contents

DEDICATION

To my daughters,

May you never settle. May you always lead with wisdom, protect your peace, and know your worth without question.

You are not the love you have received, you are the love you carry.

And to every woman who still believes in real love, this is your reset.

This is your roadmap.
This is your reminder that wanting a husband is not desperation-it's divine.

This book is for you.

The healed you.
The healing you.
The hopeful you.

LOVE,
Mom

Before the First Move

"Wisdom observes before it advances."

DEFINITIONS MATTER:

LET'S GET CLEAR INTENTIONAL DATING: Intentional dating is dating with purpose, direction, and discernment.

It means you are dating to build, not just to bond. You're not here to kill time, fill space, or feel good in the moment. You are here to observe, ask the hard questions, reflect deeply, and choose someone who aligns with your future, not just your feelings.

Intentional dating is a spiritual, emotional, and mental commitment to guard your heart while learning someone else's. It's not always deep and heavy, but it's never careless. You're paying attention to energy, habits, values, lifestyle, and how someone shows up.

CASUAL DATING: Casual dating is surface-level dating.

It's emotionally unsafe (Basically, it's when your heart and mind don't feel protected in a relationship). Spiritually draining. It's how people waste years on "situationships," distractions, and people who were never meant to go the distance.

Casual dating often includes:

- No clear direction
- Unspoken expectations
- Emotional confusion
- Physical involvement with no foundation

Nothing about dating should be casual-not your mind, body, spirit, nor your soul, nor your peace, nor your time, nor your alignment.

WHY THIS MEANS SO MUCH TO ME:

No one ever taught me how to live an intentional life. I didn't grow up hearing things like "guard your heart," or "ask questions before giving your body". I learned through pain. Through mistakes. Through trauma. Through trial and error.

That's why I get so triggered (it's when the past crashes into the present, and your mind and body react like you're still in that old situation.) when people throw around the word "casual." Because I know what it cost me to unlearn it. I know what it feels like to be wrapped up with someone who never had intentions for you-and then wonder why you're spiritually and emotionally exhausted. So, before we go any further, I need you to hear this: You deserve to date with clarity with confidence with protection with purpose. that begins with defining the standard.THIS IS WHY I WROTE

THIS BOOK. I was never taught what to look for in a man. All I was ever told as a little girl was: "Boys will say anything to get in your pants." Now I'm telling you: Don't let desire make you blind. Don't let loneliness make you foolish. And don't let a broken man convince you to break yourself to love him.

CLARITY IS NOT COLD.
STANDARDS ARE NOT SELFISH.
AND INTENTION IS HOW LOVE STAYS SAFE.

Setting the Board

Why Intentional Dating Requires Strategy, Not Chance

This book was birthed from trauma, culture, confusion & casual connections that were never meant to be anything more than a lesson. For all the people from broken households who are now grown people still walking around with childhood wounds, calling it love. Let me be clear-this is not an attack on men. This is not about shaming, blaming, or finger-pointing. This is about separating the boys from the men. Let me also say, just because you're a boy now, doesn't mean you can't grow into a man. The growth has to be something you want. That healing has to be something you choose. Maturity has to be something you pursue on your own. I'm not a man, so I can't tell you how to be one. But I do know how I should be loved by one. How I should be spoken to, covered, protected, prioritized, and pursued. And that, Queen, is enough. I know this will ruffle some feathers. I know some people will argue with this. I didn't write this for arguments; I wrote it for clarity. For the women like me who were tired of cycles, confusion, being strong for everybody, and still going home feeling unseen. If this book makes you pause, reflect, cry, or heal-then it's already doing what it was created to do.

POSTURE OF THE HEART

When dating with purpose, especially if you're seeking a relationship rooted in faith, a relationship with God ensures you're walking with wisdom, not flesh. Meaning that your standards and decisions aren't driven by emotion or loneliness, but by discernment and alignment with God's will. Meanwhile, a heart postured toward God keeps you humble, honest, and pure in your intentions. The reason you are dating is not to fill a void or prove something, but because you're ready to love the right way; selflessly, maturely, and with clarity. Lastly, being God-fearing creates accountability. It shapes how you treat others, how you respond to conflict, and how you uphold boundaries and honor the process. Without reverence for God, it's easy to justify behavior that leads to heartbreak or confusion.

Posture of the Heart

This refers to the condition, attitude, and motives of your inner self. It refers to your character, your humility, your willingness to love, forgive, obey, and submit to God. It's not about what you say but what you live. A heart that's postured toward God is open, teachable, accountable, and aligned with His will.

Relationship with God

Having a relationship with God means you actively communicate with Him, spend time in His Word, seek His guidance, and walk with Him daily. It's personal, intimate, and growing; not just religious rituals, but a real connection that shapes how you live and make decisions.

God-Fearing

Being God-fearing doesn't mean being scared of God; it means revering, honoring, and respecting Him enough to obey His Word, even when it's hard. It's having a holy fear that keeps you from doing anything that would displease Him, not out of fear of punishment, but out of love and reverence. If god matters most to you ask him if he has a relationship with God and is he God fearing (not do he know him or believe) if the answer he provides is answer are no or anything but a solid yes, he will hurt you intentionally and unintentionally.

UNDERSTANDING RED FLAGS & GREEN FLAGS

Let's break it down, dating world style. In the streets and in real-world dating, a red flag is a warning.

MEANING: DO NOT PASS GO. DO NOT COLLECT ANYTHING. DO NOT INVEST.

That red light means stop, protect yourself, and leave him ALONE! It doesn't matter how cute, charming, or smooth he appears to be; a red flag signals harm. Eventually, it will cost you something, and the collateral damage left behind is very, very hard to repair.

On the flip side...A green flag means GO! This is someone who is self-aware, emotionally available, respectful, and aligned with where you're headed. It doesn't mean they're perfect, but it means they're showing consistency and honesty. If you're ignoring red flags, soul ties are probably in play. Once intimacy enters the picture, clarity usually exits. Effort. Green doesn't mean "marry them tomorrow"- it means "you're safe to get to know them further."

I know you're probably wondering, what's a soul tie? Soul ties can be unhealthy, but God created them for his divine purpose. Let's talk about them because they're real and they run deep.

A soul tie is a strong connection between you and another person. It can form through sex, deep conversations, emotional bonding, shared trauma, or spiritual experiences. It's more than just a feeling; it's a link that can impact your thoughts, behaviors, and emotions long after the relationship has changed or ended.

Healthy Soul Ties

These are the connections that uplift, strengthen, and align with God's purpose. They're built on love, truth, respect, and accountability. A strong marriage rooted in faith can create a healthy soul tie. Deep friendships that sharpen and support you can, too. These ties help you grow, heal, and feel safe.

Unhealthy Soul Ties

These are formed when we connect deeply with someone through sex, trauma, or emotional dependency outside of God's order, especially when there's manipulation, toxicity, or confusion involved. You can't let them go, even when you know they're bad for you. You ignore red flags because you feel "tied" to them. You keep reliving the bond emotionally, spiritually, or sexually— even when you're physically apart.

Unhealthy soul ties are like chains: they drain your peace, cloud your judgment, and keep you stuck in cycles of pain, regret, or obsession.

Truth is, some of us aren't in love; we're just tied. And until you recognize the difference, you'll keep mistaking pain for purpose and bondage for love. Breaking soul ties takes intentional healing, prayer, and often deliverance. You have to reclaim your soul and give it back to God piece by piece.

Here's the key:

Red and green flags don't always scream; some whisper. That's why this manual is built around discernment-so you don't miss the whispers while getting distracted by the charm.

HOW MANY RED FLAGS DO YOU NEED?

A word from my therapist changed my life... "How many red flags do you need to collect before you realize this person is not your person? How many do you need, Eclesia, before you end up with a circus baby?" Whewwww. That hit me in my chest. We've all ignored red flags. We've all said, "Well, maybe he'll grow out of it," or "But he has potential." But potential does not equal preparation, and charm does not equal character. Now, I challenge you: Sit back and reflect: What are your deal breakers? Not what you tell him in a "get to know you" text... Not what you sugarcoat on the first date... I mean, deep down, what are the things that are an absolute NO for you?

Just a sample of some of my deal breakers:

- Not being established at 35+

Explanation: A car, a stable job, a home. If you haven't prioritized your life, how will you prioritize me?

- Poor hygiene

 Explanation: You don't have to be polished head to toe, but you shouldn't be musty (body odor), crusty (ashy, dry skin), or dirty (visible stains, dirty nails). Self-respect is visible

- No self-care or discipline

Explanation: His lifestyle reflects chaos. I already know what I'd be stepping into. Because hear me: If a man doesn't love himself, he will not know how to love you.

- No Hobbies

Explanation: Having hobbies before entering a relationship fosters self-identity, emotional balance, and independence. Hobbies help avoid codependency while nurturing a healthier, more resilient connection.

REFLECTION PROMPT: My Deal Breakers

Write out the top 3-5 things you can't ignore, excuse, or entertain in your next relationship.

____

____

____

____

____

____

Self-Check

We jumping straight off the porch, without me holding you accountable for how you are entering the dating world.

Before you call yourself intentionally dating, please make sure you're in a place of healing. Not healed all the way. Not perfect. But grounded. Focused. Whole enough not to attract what will break you again.

- You can't date with clarity when your emotions are in crisis.
- You can't choose wisely when your life is in shambles.
- You can't build with someone when you're still rebuilding yourself.

At the very least, before dating intentionally:

- You need a stable mind.
- You need a safe place to live.
- You need a consistent stream of income.
- You need peace, not panic, in your spirit.

A HARD TRUTH FOR MY DESPERATE WOMEN:

Yes, there are plenty of men in the sea. But don't you dare go fishing for a project. Youare not here to build a man: You are here to build with one. He is a man. Which means that he should already be operating in leadership. A man is a protector, a provider, a covering-not someone you need to rescue. Do we all need help sometimes? Yes. But you are not his God, & he is not your God either, at this big age? He should have some level of stability, financially, mentally, and emotionally.

Ask Yourself:

Would he pause his life and wait for you to get yourself together?

____

____

____

____

____

____

Do you even like him that much to be his rehab center?

____

____

____

____

____

Or... did you jump the gun and give him your body before you got to know his character?

____

____

____

____

____

POSITION MATTERS:
WOMEN ARE NOT SEEKERS. WE ARE RESPONDERS.

As women, we are divinely designed to respond, not chase, not initiate, not lead in pursuit. Please be mindful of the environment you are responding to. Where you meet someone matters. If your introduction begins in chaos, confusion, or compromise, don't be surprised when the connection reflects that energy. Let's step back and process this now. The way something starts often sets the tone for how it will go.

If you meet someone during a messy time in your life, or theirs, where there's a lot of drama, secrets, mixed signals, or you have to go against your values just to keep their attention, then the relationship is already starting on shaky ground. That energy doesn't magically go away. It usually grows.

Chaos might look like fighting early, situation ships, or third parties already in the picture.

Confusion might be you not knowing where you stand, feeling unsure, getting mixed signals, or constantly second-guessing yourself.

Compromise is when you shrink yourself, ignore your standards, or settle just to keep the person.

When you ignore the mess at the beginning, that same mess will likely show up later, just in different forms. The energy you allow in the beginning sets the pace for everything that follows. So, if you started by sacrificing peace, don't be shocked when peace is always missing.

I began to realize: It's not just who you date, but where you meet them and how you respond that sets the tone.

I do not recommend dating apps, DMs, or random texts from strangers.

From personal experience, I've learned that in-person encounters rooted in peace, alignment, and mutual energy are best.

Look for healthy meeting places:

- Classes
- Church
- Networking events
- Volunteer opportunities
- Gym
- Conferences or interest-based gatherings

Avoid first connections from:

- Clubs
- Bars
- Gas stations
- Liquor stores
- Random inboxes

Your environment reflects your energy, and your energy sets the tone for what (and who) you attract.

CHAPTER 1

The Opening Move

"So, Tell Me a Little Bit About Yourself."

"Every game reveals itself in the opening."

Intentional dating begins with observation, not assumption.

Intentional dating is like a job interview for your lifelong partner, and the position is permanent.. This isn't about being casual; it's about connection, clarity, and compatibility. You're not just mingling bodies. You're mingling spirits, goals, emotions, and peace. That's not light work.

Remove the idea of "casual" from your vocabulary when it comes to dating with purpose.

This question opens the door to everything: who they are, what they've done, how they see themselves, and how they use their time. Purpose requires clarity.

What to Watch For on the Board

Red Flags:

- They only lead with achievements.
- No hobbies or signs of joy.
- Vague or inconsistent job history.
- Every role they've ever had is authoritative or entrepreneurial without success.

Green Flags:

- Balance of work and life.
- Authentic self-awareness. (accountability being real with oneself)
- Emotional and spiritual depth.

"Above all else, guard your heart, for everything you do flows from it."

                    Proverbs 4:23

Reading the Board

When someone asks you to describe yourself, what do you lead with? Why?

____

____

____

____

____

What are three things you should listen for in someone else's answer?

____

____

____

____

Have you ever overlooked red flags in a person's self-description?

____

____

____

____

____

Make a chart: past person - what they said vs. what they showed.

WHO	SAID	SHOWN

Prayer: "God, help me guard my heart and recognize character beyond charisma."

Every game is decided early. Pay attention.

CHAPTER 2

Developing the Pieces
"What Are Your Short-Term Goals?"

"The plans of the diligent lead surely to abundance."

What are your short-term goals?

This question lets you know if someone is actively working on their life, or if they're stuck in survival mode. A short-term goal reveals direction, focus, and drive. It informs you on whether they're floating or building.

What to Watch For on the Board

Red Flags:

- No goals at all.
- Goals are vague or sound rehearsed.
- Same goals for the past 5 years with no movement.

Green flags:

- Realistic goals.
- Reasonable timelines.
- Achievable steps.

Mini Eggshell Tip:

Don't ask this on a loud, distracting date.
Wait for a calm conversation, phone, park, or quiet ride.

"The plans of the diligent lead surely to abundance, but everyone who is hasty comes only to poverty."

Proverbs 21:5

Assessing the Position

List three short-term goals you've set.

____

____

____

____

What red flag answers would you now recognize?

____

____

____

____

What's the difference between planning and pretending?

____

____

____

Prayer: "Lord, help me align with people who plan, pursue, and prepare.

Direction reveals intention.

CHAPTER THREE

Seeing the Whole Board
"What Are Your Long-Term Goals?"

"Vision decides the end before the first move is finished

What Are Your Long-Term Goals?

This question shows whether they have vision.

People who are mentally or emotionally unstable usually can't see the future clearly because survival mode keeps the focus on right now. A person with healing, hope, and direction will speak about what's next with intention.

Long-term goals show whether a person is planning a life or just reacting to circumstances. Vision doesn't have to be flashy, but it does have to be grounded. Dreams without structure are just fantasies.

What the Board Reveals

Red Flags:

- No clarity on the future
- Unrealistic fantasies with no strategy
- Saying what sounds good but lacks evidence

Green Flags:

- Should build on short-term goals
- Vision with structure
- Purpose over performance

Example of a short-term goal that was built in the direction of a long-term goal:

Someone looking to build in real estate or residual income would say, "I already own a home, and I'm working toward investing in rental properties in the next 3-5 years."

"The wise store up choice food and olive oil, but fools gulp theirs down."

Proverbs 21:20

Playing the Long Game

What does your long-term future look like?

____

____

____

____

____

Have you confused potential with actual planning?

____

____

____

____

____

Do you attract dreamers or doers?

____

____

____

Prayer: "God, anchor my steps and align me with legacy-minded people."

Vision isn't loud. It's deliberate.

CHAPTER FOUR

The Mirror Test

"Do You Have Any Flaws?"

"Growth begins where honesty lives."

Do You Have Any Flaws? If so, what are they?

This reveals emotional intelligence, humility, and growth. If someone says they have no flaws, they lack accountability and awareness. Nobody is perfect. If you say you are, you're not ready for partnership (past girl over here if he says no flaws means he thinks he's perfect, everything that goes wrong will be your fault, wink).

A person who is prepared for partnership understands that growth is ongoing. They don't hide from their weaknesses. They take responsibility for them.

What the Board Reveals

Red Flags:

- "I've worked on all my flaws."
- "I don't really have any."
- Avoids giving an example
-Blaming others for their struggles or circumstances for personal struggles

Green Flag:

- "I'm actively working on it."
- "This is something I've become more mindful of."
- It's a process, but I've gotten better over time."

Example of growth awareness:

"I struggle with time management, but I've started using a planner."

That answer shows ownership, effort, and maturity.

"Examine yourselves to see whether you are in the faith; test yourselves. Do you not realize that Christ Jesus is in you unless, of course, you fail the test?"

2 Corinthians 13:5

The Mirror Square

What flaw are you aware of and working on?

____

____

____

____

____

How do you respond when someone gives you feedback?

____

____

____

____

____

Do you own your flaws or deflect them?

____

____

____

Prayer: "Lord, teach me to grow and to recognize people who are committed to growth."

You can't grow what you won't examine.

CHAPTER FIVE

Inherited Patterns
"How's Your Relationship With Your Family?"

"You don't inherit peace. You learn how to build it."

How's Your Relationship with Your Family?

This question reveals family trauma, healing, and boundaries.

You'll know whether someone is emotionally safe or still wounded. If someone who dumps all their family's business on you without grace is a red flag, moreover someone who sugarcoats everything might be hiding/covering something, too.

What to Watch For on the Board

Red Flags:

- "My whole family is toxic."
- "I can't stand none of them."
- Savior complex: "Everyone depends on me."

Green flags:
- "We had our ups and downs, but I've learned to set boundaries."
- "It's complicated, but I've found peace in how I show up."
- "I value my family, but I won't let dysfunction define me."

Healthy Response:

For my peace, I've separated from family, but I love and pray for them.

"If it is possible, as far as it depends on you, live at peace with everyone."

Romans 12:18

Prayer: "God, give me peace with my past and clarity about the people I allow into my present."

"Lord, help me heal from the pain of my past and set healthy boundaries with love. Teach me to honor others without losing myself. Amen

Spot the Pattern

What does your current family dynamic look like?

____

____

____

____

____

How do you talk about your upbringing?

____

____

____

____

____

What red flags have you seen in others' family responses?

____

____

____

____

You don't have to repeat the path you were given.

CHAPTER SIX

Defining the Win
"What Does Love Look Like to You?"

"Love is more than a feeling. It's an action."

What Does Love Look Like to You?

Love isn't something we automatically know. Love is learned. Love is taught sometimes in toxic ways. What someone says about love will reveal their inner script and past experiences. expectations, wounds, and examples. Love, as they understand it, will shape how they show up, how they treat you, and what they tolerate.

Pay attention to the language they use.
Love without accountability is just a feeling.
Love without action is just a story.

What the Board Reveals

Red Flags:
- Trash-talking exes.
- "I've never been loved right," but takes no accountability.
- They can't define love or link it to action.

Green flags:
- Respect
- Commitment
- Give and Take

"Love is patient, love is kind. It does not envy, it does not boast, it is not proud. It does not dishonor others, it is not self-seeking, it is not easily angered, it keeps no record of wrongs. Love does not delight in evil but rejoices with the truth. It always protects, always trusts, always hopes, always perseveres. Love never fails. But where there are prophecies, they will cease; where there are tongues, they will be stilled; where there is knowledge, it will pass away."

1 Corinthians 13:4-8

Prayer: "God, show me love through Your eyes, not my past wounds."

36

Check Your Alignment

What does love look like for you today?

____

____

____

____

____

What's your love language?

____

____

____

____

____

What did love look like in your past relationships?

____

____

____

____

Exercise: Replace the word "love" with their name in
1 Corinthians. If it doesn't feel right, trust that.

Hold on now, we can't be asking people what love is, and we don't know. So, below is a clear, definitive outline of what love is.

WHAT IS LOVE, REALLY?

We talk a lot about self-love, which is good. However, as a babe in Christ, I've learned this: We can't love ourselves properly until we know how God loves us. The truth is, some of us have never truly loved ourselves.

-We've survived.
-We've hustled.
-We've performed.
-We've "put on" to feel worthy.

But we've never learned how to care for ourselves the way God commands us to. If we don't love ourselves the right way, we'll never love someone else the right way either.

"Love the Lord your God with all your heart, soul, and mind... and love your neighbor as yourself."

Matthew 22:37-39

WHAT IS LOVE?

Love is not just a feeling.
Love is action, sacrifice, consistency, correction, covering, discipline, and honor.

WHAT IS SELF-LOVE?

Self-love is not selfish-it's sacred, as long as God is at the center. There's nothing wrong with being rooted in self-love, as long as it's not self-driven, rooted in ego, and arrogant. God must be in the midst of it.

Self-love means:

- I protect my peace.
- I set boundaries.
- I speak to myself with grace.
- I forgive myself for what I didn't know.
- I treat my body with care.
- I stop letting broken people define my worth.
- I heal my soul with God-not people.

If you love others more than you love yourself, you'll settle and people-please. If you love yourself more than you love God, you'll become prideful. When you love God first, He teaches you how to love both properly (self & others). That's why love starts at the altar, not in a bedroom.

REMINDER FOR YOUR INTENTIONAL QUESTIONS:

Don't be afraid to dig deeper.
Ask clarifying questions.
Ask follow-up for patterns.
Watch their body language, because this person could potentially shape your future-and that should never be approached passively.

Prayer: Lord, teach me what real love looks like, starting with Your love. Heal every place in me that confused pain for love, and help me to love myself the way You love me, so I can love others with truth, wisdom, and grace. Amen.

CHAPTER SEVEN

The Anchor Question
"Do You Want to Be in a Relationship?"

"Clarity chooses before confusion costs you."

Do you want to be in a Relationship?

This is the anchor.

Ask this directly. If they've made it this far, their answer will either give you clarity or expose confusion.

Red Flags:
- "Just vibing, going with the flow."
- "I don't believe in labels."
- "I'll know when I know."

Green flags:
-I would love a partner
-Can't wait to have a wife
-I don't like wasting time (kind of a yellow)

Let's dig deeper into the yellow. When someone says, "I don't like wasting time," it sounds good at first, but be careful. It's a yellow flag because it can mean a few different things.

Sometimes people say this to rush things or get what they want without being honest about their true intentions. It can be used to manipulate, make you feel guilty, or pressure you into a relationship too fast. Other times, it's coming from someone who people-pleases; they say what sounds good, but deep down, they're still unsure or unhealed. They might not be ready, but they don't want to lose you either. So, don't just listen to what they say. Watch what they do. Real intentions show over time.

Take this time to dig a little deeper.

Suggestions: ask him his thoughts and opinions on each subject, see if his answers align, teach, or inspire you.

- Marriage
- Parenting
- Roles
- Cleanliness
- Cooking
- Finances
- Schedules

Amos 3:3 "Do two walk together unless they have agreed to do so?

Choose Your Next Move

What do you want out of your next relationship?

____

____

____

____

____

What daily habits matter to you in a partner?

____

____

____

____

____

What kind of life do you want to build?

____

____

____

____

Prayer: "God, don't let me settle for confusion or convenience. Give me the courage to ask the hard questions and the wisdom to walk away from anything that isn't aligned with Your vision for my life. Lead me to someone who values partnership, purpose, and truth. Amen

PAUSE!!

Before You Move Forward

These seven questions are not casual.
They are a part of a spiritual and emotional litmus test.

They reveal whether you're engaging with a healed man
or a hurting one. A partner or a placeholder. A leader or
a liability.

These questions are not meant to interrogate.
They are meant to illuminate.

If you've made it this far, honor that.

Thank you for choosing to date with intention.
Thank you for doing the work most people avoid.
Thank you for refusing to rush what deserves
discernment.

You now have clarity. And clarity changes how you
move.

Reflective Prayer

God, thank You for wisdom, discernment, and healing.
Help me walk boldly in truth, even if that means walking
alone for a season. I trust You with my heart. Amen.

CHAPTER EIGHT

False Queens & Shiny Boards

Imagery vs. Intimacy: When the Look Matters More Than the Life

"Don't be dazzled. Be discerning."

Imagery vs. Intimacy

When the Look Matters More Than the Life

We live in a society obsessed with appearances, not reality. Big houses. Fast cars. Flashy jewelry. Designer clothes. Carefully curated social media feeds. But, behind the scenes, there's often chaos, pain, and a lack of true connection.

That, Queen, is a red flag.

When someone is obsessed with appearances, it's not just vanity. It's a form of idolatry.

It's the worship of self.
It's falling in love with how things look instead of how things are.

That's not love. That's performance.

Let's Be Real

We Love the Soft Life Too...

As women, we value beauty. We love good scents, fresh nails, quality skin care, luxury experiences, and romantic energy.

Riddle me: At what cost does that consumption come?

Are you so focused on the aesthetic that you miss the absence of authenticity?

Are you so caught up in being pampered that you're ignoring the man's principles?

A Huge Red Flag in today's Dating World:

We all know when it comes to meeting somebody new who has your attention, and you're genuinely interested in them. GURLLLL... you be on that phone caking for hours, especially in the beginning, only of course if the interest is mutual (if it's confusion it's not real) during what I like to call the honeymoon phase of dating, one of the most common things I've run across is the infamous line, "Can I just come over and chill?" That's typically the first thing out of their mouth. No planning, effort, and no protection of your space or spirit. Just "chill." Sis, that's not a date. That's a setup.

Dating with Discernment:

If a man is conversing with you and listening, he should be planning how to honor you, not how to access you. You don't need to demand the fanciest restaurant on the first date to prove your worth. Let him choose the place. Pay attention to the environment, but don't get lost in it.

Focus on him.

- How is he speaking?
- What is his body language saying?
- Does he seem centered or performative?
- Is he confident or cocky?
- Is he present or preoccupied?

BONUS:

"Let Me Come Over" Is Not a Love Language

It's a setup. When a man says, "Let me come over," early on. it's not a vibe-it's a tactic. Its how convenience becomes a contract-without your consent.

Once you open that door, here's what you unknowingly agree to:

- Becoming a convenient body
- Becoming a convenient meal
- Becoming a convenient therapist
- Becoming a convenient place to escape his real life

All of that... without any commitment, covering, or care. Convenience never comes with responsibility.

That's why these men show up when it's easy, but disappear when it requires effort.

A man who's for you, who sees you, values you, and wants to build with you is not going to:

- Invite himself into your home
- Lay on your couch
- Use your Wi-Fi
- Eat your food
- Stroke his ego with your body

All within the first 90 days.

When a man is truly interested, he takes his time. He doesn't rush access. He respects boundaries; most importantly, he sees you as a responsibility, not an opportunity.

Queen, here's your reminder:

You are not a pit stop, a late-night craving, not a "slide-through." And you definitely are not a convenience or of convenience.

You are a CALLING!!

"Charm is deceptive, and beauty is fleeting; but a woman who fears the LORD is to be praised."

Proverbs 31:30

Access vs. Commitment

Where Have I Let Convenience Masquerade as Connection? What Boundaries Do I Need to Reinforce to Guard My Peace and Space?

____

____

____

____

____

____

____

____

____

____

Prayer God, help me value substance over style. Teach me to see beyond charm, looks, and effortlessness. Give me eyes to discern intention, ears to hear truth, and a heart that refuses to settle for surface. Remind me that I am not here to be consumed, I am here to be covered. Amen

CHAPTER NINE

Do Not Trade Your Queen
"Stop Selling Your Submission for a Steak"

— • —

"Submission is sacred. It's not leverage."

Stop Selling Your Submission for a Steak

"She is more precious than rubies; nothing you desire can compare with her."

Proverbs 3:15

Let's get real, just because you're on a date doesn't mean you owe anyone your body, your energy, your mind, or your soul. A meal is not a transaction. A conversation is not consent. A smile is not an invitation, interest does not mean entitled to your time, space, or energy.

Don't SELL Your Submission!!

Submission is sacred. It's not something you dangle as bait. And it's definitely not something you owe a man for taking you to dinner.

You are not on that date to prove you're worthy of love by offering sex, over-giving emotionally, or pouring out your story before it's time. Your presence, energy, and standards are enough.

Dating Tip:

Always Have Your Own Money. Yes, the man should pay because it's a sign of leadership.

But you should always offer to tip.

Here's why:
- It shows you're not entitled.
- It shows you're willing to build with him.
- It shows that you respect the service staff and care about others.
- It shows maturity, stability, and grown-woman energy.

Saying, "I got the tip," says: "I'm not here for what I can get, I'm here to connect and add value."

Now Let's Talk Boundaries:

If a man expects sex after a date, is that a red flag for you?

If not, ask yourself why.

Are you craving closeness? Are you trying to buy security with sex? Are you hoping that giving your body will guarantee a relationship?

He doesn't get access to your sacred parts just because he paid for dinner. You are not an appetizer, entrée, or dessert. You are a purpose-filled woman with depth, vision, and divine worth.

PROTECT THE QUEEN

Do I tend to feel obligated to give something after being treated?

____

____

____

____

Have I ever felt guilty for saying "no" to physical intimacy after a date?

____

____

____

____

Am I okay with not having sex early on? If not, what does that say about my attachment style or sense of value?

____

____

____

____

Prayer: Lord, remind me that I am not for sale. Teach me to honor my body, my boundaries, and my worth. Help me to walk in wisdom, not pressure, to give from overflow, not emptiness. Let every connection be filtered through Your truth, and may I never trade my value for validation. Amen."

CHAPTER TEN

Guarding the Sacred Square

"The Truth About Sex: What I Tell My Daughters"

"Child of God, you were His daughter first."

The Truth About Sex: What I Tell My Daughters!

Child of God, You are someone's daughter first before anything!

Let's talk about it. Traditionally, society feeds us women this white picket fence dream. From movies to fairy tales to quiet conversations from our parents meant to "protect" our innocence... we were raised in delusion and confusion. We were told to wait. But never told why. We were warned about getting pregnant, but never taught about soul ties, emotional trauma, or how sex bonds you to someone who might not even know how to love you.

WHAT I WASN'T TAUGHT:

I wasn't taught to save myself for marriage. I wasn't told that sex wasn't just physical. It was emotional and spiritual. That it had consequences far deeper than a pregnancy test. Now I'm grown, and now I know. And now I'm teaching my daughters differently.

WHAT I TELL MY DAUGHTERS:

Save yourself. Please try. I know it's hard. But sex is not for kids. It comes with feelings, emotions, and attachments that you might not be ready for. Go to the movies. Laugh. Skate. Enjoy your youth.

Please don't give your body away for temporary attention.

YOU CAN DATE WITHOUT HAVING SEX:

Date multiple people to observe, not to sleep with. Your identity is still forming. Don't tie yourself down to one person too early. You deserve to explore with boundaries.

Practice celibacy and abstinence as much as you can. Sexual immorality is everywhere in our culture, and soul ties are very real.

Now let's break it down...

DEFINITIONS:

Celibacy: A voluntary vow to abstain from all sexual activity, usually for spiritual or religious reasons. Abstinence: A decision to refrain from sex, either until marriage or until a specific season of life or emotional readiness.

Sexual Immorality: Any form of sexual activity outside the boundaries of God's will (which is within a covenant of marriage). This includes casual sex, porn, adultery, lust, and sexual manipulation.

"If I have sex on the first date, he won't judge me." Yes, he will. He may not say it, but it changes how he sees you. And be honest... You would judge another woman for doing it too. Your brain and emotions are trying to justify it-but you know deep down it doesn't sit right. That's the Holy Spirit checking you.

Sex too soon distorts your value-not in God's eyes, but in your own. Because once you give your body, it becomes harder to enforce your boundaries. You second-guess yourself. You stay longer. You settle faster.

YOU NEED TO KNOW THIS:

As women, we naturally release a chemical called oxytocin during sex. It's a bonding hormone. This is called "pair bonding. It makes us emotionally attached-even to someone who is not good for us. So, when you keep giving your body away too early, you keep tying your soul to men who were never assigned to your future.

"Flee from sexual immorality. All other sins a person commits are outside the body, but whoever sins sexually, sins against their own body."

1 Corinthians 6:18

What did you learn about sex growing up?

____

____

____

Have you ever connected sexually to feel loved or validated?

____

____

____

What boundaries do you need to set to protect your peace, spirit, and purpose?

____

____

____

Prayer: Father, thank You for truth. Thank You for grace. Teach me to honor my body as Your temple and protect the sacredness of my spirit. Heal every place in me that believed sex would bring love, and give me the strength to walk in purity, peace, and purpose. Help me guide others, especially my daughters, with wisdom, not shame. Amen.

CHAPTER ELEVEN

The Bonds You Can't See

"Invisible Connections That Shape the Game"

"Sex is not just physical. It's spiritual."

Sex is not just physical. It's spiritual, emotional, and psychological. When you give yourself to someone, you're also receiving who they are, including their unhealed trauma, emotional instability, and spiritual confusion.

SPIRITUAL TRANSFERENCE: Ever had sex with someone and suddenly felt sad, anxious, unfocused, or heavy? That's not just you. That's spiritual transference and is the sharing of DNA, energy, and soul essence.

You're not just connecting bodies, you're opening your soul. If they're moving in chaos, you'll feel unstable. If they're emotionally wounded, you'll start to mirror their confusion. If they're carrying spiritual baggage, you'll carry it too.

Sex opens spiritual portals. If the person you're with is not rooted, you will inherit their instability. I got to dig a little deeper so you can understand the severity of granting an unhealed man your body. It's not just physical; it connects your spirit to theirs. So, if he is lost, broken, confused, or full of drama... some of that can get on you, too. You might start feeling anxious, depressed, angry, or just not like yourself, and not know why. It's because his energy, his demons, his battles, you picked some of it up.

If he is not rooted in God, not healed, or not whole, you can end up carrying stuff that was never yours to begin with. That's why who you sleep with matters. It's not just your body, it's your soul that's involved.

EMOTIONAL IMPACT

When sex is used to feel loved, seen, or validated, it leaves deep emotional bruises. You begin to equate intimacy with acceptance, even when you're not being honored. You may feel anxious, clingy, or abandoned after sex because your emotions were never safe to begin with. Your ability to trust your instincts becomes foggy, and your self-worth starts to shrink. Over time, you may confuse chemistry with compatibility and mistake attention for affection.

PSYCHOLOGICAL IMPACT

Repeated sexual connections, especially outside of commitment, can distort your mental clarity. You may experience cognitive dissonance, knowing it's not right, but still craving the person. You might stay longer in toxic relationships because of the bond that's been built through sex. You begin to doubt your value, thinking you have to give more to keep someone interested. This creates a cycle of giving too much, too soon, hoping it will finally be enough.

"Do you not know that he who unites himself with a prostitute is one with her in body? For it is said, "The two will become one flesh.""

1 Corinthians 6:16

Prayers: God, break every invisible bond that was never from You. Heal my soul from what I allowed in moments of confusion and longing. Restore my mind, emotions, and spirit. Help me walk in discipline and discernment, and teach me to guard my temple like the sacred space it is. Amen.

WHAT ARE YOU DEFENDING?

Have you ever had sex with son one and found yourself procrastinating?

____

____

Have you ever had sex with someone and felt extremely sad or disinterested a few days later?

____

____

Have you ever had sex with someone and instantly felt disgusted?

____

____

Have you ever kept sleeping with someone you knew wasn't good for you, but couldn't seem to stop?

____

____

After being intimate, did you ever feel confused about your feelings or second-guess your own worth?

____

____

Have you ever felt like sex was the only way to feel close to someone who barely gave you anything else?

____

____

____

Do you notice your emotions change when they change, even if nothing is said out loud?

____

____

____

Have you ever stayed in a toxic situation because the sex made it harder to walk away?

____

____

____

Do you feel like you've been "giving" your body in hopes of being chosen, loved, or kept?

____

____

____

Have you ever ignored God's voice, or your own gut, because the connection felt too strong to let go?

____

____

____

____

____

____

CHAPTER TWELVE

Holding the Line

Boundaries & Discernment: Your First Line of Protection

"Protection is wisdom in motion."

Boundaries & Discernment:
Your First Line of Protection

WHAT IS A BOUNDARY?

A boundary is a line you draw to protect your peace, purpose, and your spirit. A deal breaker protects you from long-term damage. A boundary protects you from everyday harm.

MY BREAKTHROUGH:

I used to overextend myself. As a people-pleaser and "Captain Save Everybody," I always said yes-even when my plate was already full.

In dating, overextending looks like:
- Being too available too soon
- Sharing too much too early
- Offering your resources before trust is earned
- Saying "yes" to help when your "no" would protect you

THE FIRST BOUNDARY: LEARN TO SAY NO

No is complete. It doesn't need justification or guilt. Be bold, clear & still.

RED FLAG:
- When a man offers money, gifts, or favors right away, it may seem generous.

But ask yourself:
- What is this tied to?
- Is he buying my body or investing in my heart?

Most of the time, instant generosity is rooted in lust, not love.

Healthy Signs in Boundaries & Discernment

- They respect your "no" without pushing back or guilt tripping

Explanation: They respect your "no" without pressure: You say, "I'm not ready." They say, "Okay, I understand." You say, "I don't want to go." They say, "No problem." You say, "I'm not comfortable with that."

- They don't argue or make you feel bad.

Explanation: You say, "Not tonight." They don't pout, ignore you, or try to guilt you.

Real respect doesn't need convincing. If someone keeps pushing, that's not respect, it's control.

-They ask what you're comfortable with, physically, emotionally, spiritually.
-They take their time to get to know you before expecting access.
-They listen and adjust when you express a need or concern.

"All you need to say is simply 'Yes' or 'No'; anything beyond this comes from the evil one."

Matthew 5:37

Prayer: God, help me recognize what's real and release what's not. Teach me to set boundaries that reflect my healing, not my fear. Let me walk boldly in discernment, knowing that my peace is not negotiable. Remove anyone sent to distract, drain, or derail me, and align me with those who walk in truth, honor, and respect. Help me protect my value, preserve my energy, and remember that saying 'no' is one of the greatest ways I can say 'yes' to You. Amen

What's one boundary you wish you had enforced sooner?

\
\

Where do you tend to overextend-emotionally, financially, or physically?

\
\

How can you honor your "no" without guilt starting today?

\
\

Have you ever connected sexually to feel loved or validated?

\
\

What boundaries do you need to set to protect your peace, spirit, and purpose?

____

____

____

____

____

Queen, if you've made it to the end of this book, I want you to know: you are no longer the woman who started it. You've confronted hard truths. You've examined your patterns. You've peeled back layers of pain, desire, fear, and faith.

That alone makes you brave. You didn't just read a book, you committed to healing. You allowed wisdom to lead where your wounds used to be. This journey wasn't about finding a man. It was about finding yourself. Let this be your reset. Your reminder. Your road back to purpose.

You don't need to beg to be loved. You don't need to perform to be kept. You don't need to shrink to be chosen. You are the prize because God says so.

When you truly believe that, you'll stop entertaining anything that makes you forget it.

Final Blessing, I pray your standards stay firm, even when you're lonely. I pray that your boundaries protect you, even when they're tested. Also, that your healing runs so deep that broken love no longer feels familiar.

The next time love shows up... it should look like peace, feel like safety, and sound like God. You are worthy of real love, intentional love, Kingdom love. And when it arrives? You'll recognize it. Because this time...you're ready.

WITH LOVE,

Eclesia Holmes

GLOSSARY

THE LANGUAGE OF THE GAME

Abstinence

A personal decision to refrain from sexual activity for a period of time or until a specific standard is met, such as marriage, emotional readiness, or spiritual alignment.

Accountability

The willingness to take responsibility for one's actions, choices, patterns, and growth without blaming others or making excuses.

Attachment Style

The emotional patterns that influence how a person bonds, connects, and responds in relationships are often shaped by early experiences and trauma.

Boundaries

Clear limits set to protect your peace, purpose, body, emotions, time, and spirit. Boundaries define what behavior is acceptable and what is not.

Casual Dating

Surface-level dating without intention, clarity, or commitment often leads to emotional confusion, misalignment, and unprotected attachment.

Celibacy

A voluntary commitment to abstain from all sexual activity, often for spiritual, healing, or faith-based reasons.

Chemistry

Emotional or physical attraction that feels intense but does not necessarily indicate compatibility, safety, or long-term alignment.

GLOSSARY

Compatibility

The alignment of values, goals, communication styles, faith, lifestyle, and vision for the future.

Convenience

When access to someone's time, body, energy, or emotional labor is prioritized over commitment, effort, or responsibility.

Deal Breaker

A non-negotiable standard or condition that, if violated, disqualifies someone from continued dating or partnership.

Discernment

Spiritual and emotional wisdom that allows you to perceive truth beyond words, charm, or appearances.

Emotional Availability

The capacity to communicate feelings, handle conflict, and build intimacy in a healthy, consistent way.

Emotional Intelligence

The ability to recognize, understand, and manage one's emotions while responding thoughtfully to others.

Green Flag

A sign of emotional health, maturity, accountability, alignment, or readiness for intentional partnership.

Healing

The ongoing process of addressing past trauma, wounds, and unhealthy patterns to live and love more fully.

GLOSSARY

Idolatry (in Dating)

Placing excessive value on appearance, status, money, or validation above character, faith, and truth.

Intentional Dating

Dating with purpose, clarity, and discernment to build a healthy, aligned partnership rather than pass time or seek validation.

Leadership

Demonstrated responsibility, consistency, initiative, and the ability to provide direction, protection, and stability.

Lust

Desire driven primarily by physical attraction without regard for emotional, spiritual, or relational consequences.

Pair Bonding

The emotional and chemical attachment formed through sexual intimacy is largely influenced by the release of oxytocin.

People-Pleaser

Someone who prioritizes others' approval over their own needs, boundaries, or well-being.

Red Flag

A warning sign indicating emotional immaturity, misalignment, manipulation, instability, or lack of readiness for partnership.

Self-Abandonment

Ignoring personal needs, values, or boundaries in order to maintain connection, approval, or proximity to another person.

GLOSSARY

Self-Love

Caring for yourself with discipline, compassion, and respect under God's guidance, not ego or pride.

Situationship

An undefined romantic or sexual connection lacking clarity, commitment, or agreed-upon direction.

Soul Tie

A deep emotional or spiritual bond formed through intimacy, shared trauma, or prolonged connection that can be healthy or unhealthy.

Spiritual Transference

The emotional and spiritual exchange that occurs through intimacy, where one person absorbs another's unresolved pain, energy, or instability.

Submission

A sacred expression of trust, respect, and partnership that is given freely, not owed, traded, or coerced.

Validation

Seeking worth, approval, or identity through attention, affection, or intimacy rather than through God and self-awareness.

Vision

The ability to see, plan, and prepare for a future with clarity, structure, and purpose.

ABOUT THE AUTHOR

I am a woman who learned how to listen long before the world taught me how to speak up.

Yes, I am a mother of five, and motherhood has deeply shaped me. Two of my children are autistic. One is nonverbal. The other is high-functioning. Their experiences live on the same spectrum, yet show up in completely different ways. Through them, I learned that communication is not always spoken. It's expressed through facial expressions, gestures, sounds, patterns, and energy. My nonverbal child doesn't use words, but he is always communicating. You just have to slow down enough to learn his language.

My high-functioning child speaks and manages many daily tasks, but that doesn't mean life is effortless. She navigates social situations, emotional regulation, changes in routine, and the pressure of masking just to appear "normal." From the outside, it may look like she's fine. Inside, she may be managing anxiety, sensory overload, or exhaustion. Parenting both of them taught me something I carry into every area of my life: different doesn't mean less. It simply means different.

I have three daughters, ages 21, 19, and 14, and two sons, ages 16 and 9. I've had children by three different men, and I spent thirteen years in one long-term relationship, from 2009 to 2022. What some people experience across multiple relationships, I experienced within one. Over time, we grew apart. The ending was painful and deeply traumatic. It took therapy, prayer, and surrendering to God to release the bitterness and find my way back to peace.

When I stepped back into dating, I was thirty-four years old. I had been with the same man since I was twenty. I was new to dating. New to the streets. New to the games. New to the red flags. And new to the realization that love isn't enough without alignment.

I ignored my intuition more times than I want to admit. I answered random "hey" messages. Entertained good mornings that led nowhere. Held onto hope that someone might surprise me. Most men weren't offering love. They were offering lust. Looking for somewhere to place their bodies, not somewhere to plant their spirit.

That's how this book was born.

Through tears. Through prayer. Through failed conversations and gut instincts, I should've honored sooner. I began to understand that it's not just who you date, but where you meet them and how you respond that sets the tone. I learned how to recognize red flags within the first five minutes of a conversation. I learned how to ask questions that reveal whether a man is simply performing or actually preparing to build something real.

No, I haven't met my intentional partner yet.

But what I've gained in the process is clarity, discernment, and self-trust. And now, I'm passing that wisdom on to you. Not from a place of perfection, but from lived experience. From a woman who learned the hard way. And chose to learn intentionally.

EVERY MOVE MATTERS.
CHOOSE WITH INTENTION.

www.ingramcontent.com/pod-product-compliance
Lightning Source LLC
Chambersburg PA
CBHW061352140726
47997CB00003B/1176